1

A CIP catalogue record for this book is available from the British Library

ISBN 0 9527638 0 X

Typeset and printed by MFP Design & Print, Manchester

We are grateful to the Scarborough Evening News
for permission to reprint their reports of Seamer Fair

Published by FIDO PUBLISHING
Appleby-in-Westmorland, Cumbria CA16 6BD

THE APPLEBY RAI

Travelling people on a thousand-year journey
Words by Gordon Thorburn
Photographs by John Baxter

Dedication
To Joseph Noel Crackles,
gentleman of modest habits,
who will one day have a book all to himself
and has the credit for starting this one off;
and to all the gypsies who ever came to Appleby New Fair.

Contents

4

AS YOU LIKE IT V iii.

First Page: *Well met, honest gentleman.*

Touchstone: *By my troth, well met. Come sit, sit, and a song.*

Second Page: *We are for you; sit i' th' middle.*

First Page: *Shall we clap into't roundly, without hawking, or spitting, which are the only prologues to a bad voice?*

Second Page: *I'faith, i'faith; and both in tune, like two gypsies on a horse.*

WILLIAM SHAKESPEARE C.1595

ANTONY AND CLEOPATRA IV xii.

Antony: *O this false soul of Egypt! this grave charm Whose eye becked forth my wars and called them home — Whose bosom was my crownet, my chief end — Like a right gypsy hath, at fast and loose, Beguiled me to the very heart of loss.*

WILLIAM SHAKESPEARE C.1605

I'm the Romani rai
I'm a true didikai,
I build all my castles beneath the blue sky.
I live in a tent and I pay out no rent,
And that's why they call me the Romani rai.
  Kakka chavvi, dick akai,
  Father's gone to sell a mush a kushti grai,
  And that's why they call him the Romani rai.
I'm the Romani rai,
Just an old didikai,
My home is a mansion beneath the blue sky.
I was born in a ditch so I'll never grow rich,
And that's why they call me the Romani rai.

This gypsy children's song is in *pogadi jib*, or 'broken language', the blend of colloquial English with a few words of Romanes which is all that remains in modern Britain of one of the oldest living languages in the world.

Rai means 'lord', and is presumably from the same ancient root word which gives the French 'roi' and the English 'royal'.

Didikai, absorbed into ordinary English as diddicoy, a dismissive description of the gypsy lower classes, actually means a 'you get what you see' kind of chap, someone who is rough but ready (literally, a 'look here man').

Kakka chavvi, dick akai means something like 'Shush, child, and watch out'. *Grai* is a horse, and *kushti* has no English equivalent except in slang and advertising copy. Kushti is the real OK thing, a kind of Romani, secular equivalent of the Jewish kosher.

Mush is a man, and if the grai really was kushti then the mush in the song was probably a *Rom*. Otherwise, the mush would likely be a *gadjo*, that is, anybody outside the greater gypsy family.

Every gypsy is brought up to believe a central truth about every gadjo (sometimes *gaujo* or *gorgio*). Wherever you meet one, anywhere and any time in the entire universe, he is fair game.

Exceptions can be made if the gypsy knows the gadjo very well and holds him to be kushti, but even then . . .

GYPSIES

The gypsy camp was in a clearing of the forest, and consisted of one or two dirty ragged tents, a few vans, and a heterogeneous collection of old lumber scattered round, with some half starved looking dogs and bony horses and donkeys.

During the day an old woman and a few babies and young children were the only occupants of the camp, but as the shades of evening drew on, one and another, men, women and children, came in from various quarters, and active preparations for supper were commenced.

It depended very much on the "luck", or opportunities for stealing, the inhabitants had had whether this supper was bountiful or otherwise.

Sometimes the man selling clothes' pegs would produce a fine duck or chicken, or the tinker would bring out a rabbit or a joint of meat; while the women who had been fortune telling among the silly servant girls of the neighbourhood could generally produce half loaves of bread, portions of a cold joint or meat pie, to say nothing of artfully concealed bottles of spirits, without which no gypsy feast would be complete.

Then a couple of roaring fires were lighted, and big iron pots hung over them, and the various contributions of the fraternity were quickly turned into a savoury soup or stew, or if they had been out of "luck", the snails the children had gathered during the day, eked out perhaps with a hedgehog rolled in clay and baked in the fire. Gypsies are by no means particular what they eat; if they were, they would very soon starve.

When you come to Appleby New Fair and go up on the hill, look around you. See if you can spot the real gypsies, eagerly rolling hedgehogs in clay in the time honoured way, or sipping thoughtfully at their traditional snail soup.

Of the many hundreds of customers at the fortune tellers' caravans, make sure you note the proportion of silly servant girls.

The above is an extract from a novel called *The Gypsy Queen* in the British Girls' Library series, published at the turn of the century by S W Partridge & Co at one shilling and sixpence.

The author, one Emma Leslie, obviously knew her readers well and how to pander to them. She shared the British Girls' Library series with titles like *Her Bright Tomorrow* and *Rosa's Mistake*, and she shared her view of gypsies with . . . well, with whom?

That text was written about a hundred years ago. That image of gypsies, at least the image held by prissy middle-class townies like Emma Leslie, had been formed over the previous hundred years and would last pretty well intact for the next hundred, until now.

Now, every year, six or seven thousand people come to the famous Appleby gypsy fair and stay on the hill or elsewhere. They come for some of the fair, or all of it, or perhaps more than it. Of these thousands, none are in dirty ragged tents. None have half starved dogs or bony horses.

All will enjoy bountiful suppers. If it's duck tonight, contrary to popular Appleby opinion it is far more likely to have come from Cherry Valley than the well breadcrumbed banks of the river Eden.

Doubtless also there will be plenty of bottles, at supper time and all other times, artfully concealed or otherwise, but no half loaves or charitable pieces of meat pie. Why not? Why don't the gypsies on Fair Hill conform to the image? Is it because, as any resident of Appleby will tell you, only a very few of the people on the hill are "proper gypsies"?

This book is certainly not going to make pronouncements about what is a proper gypsy. The answer to that seems to depend almost entirely on where you are standing.

However, despite the paucity of hedgehog-rolling at the fair these days, the people there do seem to have a lot in common with each other. A lot of them do look like what non-gypsies think gypsies should look like. So who are they, if they're not proper?

There are few facts, some legends and a certain amount of guesswork about gypsy beginnings, and we can now have a look at all that, and then at the gypsy way of life of recent memory and romantic tale. It was a complete way of life, sufficient unto itself and it remained more or less the same for 150 years or more, before it changed so radically and recently.

The origins and early development of gypsies are not good subjects for scholars. There are no books, documents, charters or anything in writing to study, because the language and many dialects of gypsies were only ever spoken. There are no ruined buildings to reconstruct, no archaeological sites to dig up, no grave-yards, no battles for throne or territory, no burning, raping and pillaging, and there were no learned gypsy priests to chronicle the news.

Without hard evidence, historians must turn to tales that are told, and tales that are told by gypsies about themselves have been related and rerelated and passed on so many times that it would be miraculous if they bore any resemblance to the boring old truth. In any case, it would be most unusual for a gypsy, even if he knew such important truths, to give them away to an outsider.

The most unlikely story believed by some gypsies is that they sprung from Cain, son of Adam and murderer

of brother Abel. Cain was condemned to be a fugitive and a vagabond, and his sons, also doomed to live in tents, did the proper gypsy things for a living. Jubal was a musician and Tubalcain a metal worker. However, the evidence for Cain being the first gypsy gets thinner after that.

The three main names for the travellers are not much help either: Tsigani, Gypsy, and Rom.

Tsigani (Zingari in Italian, Zigeuner in German) is the name used for travellers by non-travellers in Central Europe, the Balkans and Asia Minor. It probably comes, by association, from the name of a very obscure 9th century sect called Athinganoi, who kept themselves to themselves, considered everybody else to be unclean, and made their livings by prophesy, magic and snake charming.

The other name used by European non-travellers, Gypsy (Gitano in Spain,

Gitanes on French cigarette packets), is a scornful shortening of Egyptian, and there are two possibilities for that.

Egyptian was itself a derogatory term, used long ago for anyone thought to have magical powers. Or, it could have come about because some of the early western European travellers said they had come from a country of their own called Little Egypt.

Just to confuse things even more, there is an ancient treasury called the Book of Adam, probably written around 700AD, which contains this passage:

And of the seed of Canaan were as I said the Egyptians; and lo, they were scattered all over the earth and served as the slaves of slaves.

Note that this is Canaan (Palestine) and not Cain; also that there is no other reference anywhere in history about this scattering of Egyptians going on.

While everybody else calls the travellers Tsigani or Gypsies, the travellers call themselves Romani, that is, the European ones do, and there are two possibilities for this also.

The first is that the travellers, without an historical name of their own, adopted one from the people among whom they were living at the time. Whether they saw themselves as Romans or Romanians is not clear.

The other option is linguistic. *Rom* is gypsy man (*Romni* is woman), which is said by some to be the same word as Armenian gypsy *Lom*, Palestinian gypsy *Dom*, and Sanskrit *Domba*, the name of a low caste of dancers and singers in Upper India.

Now, there is no doubt at all that the gypsy language is an old and fairly unmixed one, and that it comes from the same roots as all the modern languages now used in India and Sri Lanka.

This may or may not prove that the Roms were originally the Doms, but it surely does tell where gypsies originally came from: India. As to when they started, and how they got from India to Appleby, answers are provided mostly by guesswork and common sense.

Around the 9th and 10th centuries, life was very tough in Appleby, the rest of Westmorland, and Cumberland or southern Scotland as it sometimes was (the old border was at Penrith). Livings were extremely hard to get, and no sooner had you got something than a Viking sailed up the River Eden and took it off you or a border bandit came and set fire to it.

Presumably things were even tougher in certain parts of India at that time, because groups of people, tribes and large families, were leaving everything behind and starting a journey on foot,

with no particular place to go, no route, and no knowledge of anything which lay in front of them.

If you regard their unknown and unplanned destination as Britain, the journey would take them 600 years.

On the way, many turned aside and found their own places in the sun and rain, and they're still there, in Russia, Armenia, Moldavia, Poland, Finland, Sweden, you name it. Indeed, most of the families decided enough was enough at some point between India and UK but gradually, and largely by accident, a few of these families, greatly changed by centuries on the road, made it to the south coast of England.

Their forebears had been through Persia and Turkey, all over eastern and central Europe, into France and then across the Channel. Or, they might have gone the long way round, through Syria, Palestine, north Africa and

across to Spain. In any case, the first of the travelling people came to England in the 15th century, probably about 1435.

This is the educated guess, based on an entry in the domestic accounts of the King of Scotland in 1505. If gypsies had reached Scotland by then, presumably they had taken some considerable time to work their way through England before that.

This is what the entry says: *April 22 item; to the Egyptians by the King's command seven pounds.*

The King was James IV, a man who knew what was what, and if he paid seven pounds to some gypsies he must have been thoroughly convinced they deserved it, because that would have been like a couple of grand or more today.

Nobody knows what they did to earn such an amount. Some think it was for entertaining the King and his court with music, dancing

and fortune-telling. Probably a better guess is that they had pulled the old pilgrimage trick:

We are pilgrims from a strange land afar off, and we are on a long, er, pilgrimage, actually, through the world at the command of the, er, Pope. Yes, that's the chap. The Pope. Anyway, give us your money and earn yourself a gold star on your heavenly report card.

It's amazing how well this trick used to work, and a few months later King James was writing to his uncle, the King of Denmark, telling him about that very noble pilgrim Anthony Gagino, a Lord of Little Egypt.

The next Scottish King, James V, seems to have been even more of a sucker for gypsies. He had them dance before him in 1530, paid them forty shillings (about £600 modern equivalent) and granted them all sorts of privileges through a writ, a Privy Council writ no less, to a certain John Faw, Lord and Earl of Little Egypt.

Elsewhere the writing was not so favourable. In fact, it was on the wall. In England Henry VIII passed an Act of repression:

. . . diverse and many outlandish People calling themselves Egyptians, using no craft nor merchandise, had come into this Realm and gone from Shire to Shire and Place to Place in great Company . . . that they by Palmistry could tell men's and women's Fortunes and so many times by subtlety had deceived the People of their Money and also had committed many and heinous Felonies and Robberies to the great Hurt and Deceit of the People that they had come in among . . . From henceforth no such Person be suffered to come within this King's Realm.

"Not in my back lanes!" said the King, and he meant it. Any folk arrested as gypsies had their property confiscated and were given 15 days to get out of the country.

The basic point of contention at that time was

the same as it has been ever after. Gypsies see themselves as an elite, with a right to live off the land they pass through. By extension, they also have the right to live off non-gypsies.

If you are not a gypsy you are the Romani equivalent of a heathen, gentile sassenach. You are a gaujo, a gadjo, a gorgio, and you are there to provide whatever it is the gypsy is short of just at this very moment. The gypsy's birthright, DNA molecules and education at his mother's knee enable him to exercise his natural superiority and so to relieve his shortages as brilliantly and as often as possible.

Nowadays that generally means no more than it being perfectly OK to rip you off something rotten for your old copper water cylinder, but in days mostly gone by, it was OK to do more than rip off the gadjo. Gypsies, centuries before the French socialists, had their own

version of that founding principle of so much left-wing thought: "Property is theft" (P J Prudhon, 1840).

The gypsy version ran something like "All movable property is thievable, until it becomes a gypsy's, whereupon it is for sale."

However, no gypsy is supposed to steal from another gypsy and so, alas, they had to steal from the gadje. Logical enough. Whatever the static, orthodox population might think was the accepted thing to do, and whatever laws they might pass to govern themselves and their property, and whatever the squire might believe about his rights of ownership over wild birds, animals and fish, the travelling man did not agree.

A gypsy today could not possibly accept that it was even the most microscopic misdemeanour, much less one of Henry VIII's Heinous Felonies, for a man to park his living-wagon on a piece

of somebody else's grass, graze his horse on it, light a fire, and wade into the beck to lift a couple of trout.

16th century gypsies took the same view, but apparently extended it to include silver spoons, purses, livestock and so on.

Begging also was common, but that has never been a crime in the gypsy homeland, India. You might also argue that the Christian church was founded by a wandering beggar and is itself the biggest beggar of all time, but the worthies of Tudor England and Stuart Scotland found it a nuisance for all these gypsies to be going around begging, telling fortunes and helping themselves to fish and fowl.

By the last quarter of that century, that is from about 1575 onwards, the official view of gypsies — as eccentric entertainers with magpie tendencies — had given way to a much more virulent kind of intolerance.

Just about every European country which by now had gypsies, had also passed laws banishing them. There was nowhere left to be a gypsy.

In 1579 a new Scottish law proclaimed that:

Their ears be nailed to a tree, and cutted off, and them banished the country; and if thereafter they be found again, that they be hanged . . . the idle people calling themselves Egyptians.

In 1596 in York, gypsy children were made to watch as their parents were executed (despite Henry VIII's Act, there were 10,000 gypsies in England in Elizabeth I's time).

At Edinburgh in 1611 they hanged four Faas (still a gypsy surname, sometimes as Faw) *for abiding within the Kingdom, they being Egyptians.* A few miles away at Haddington in 1636, the Egyptians got the same shrift: *the men to be hanged and the women to be drowned, and such of the women as have children to be scourged through the burgh and burnt in the cheeks.*

These laws, dreadfully harsh although not untypical of the time, were enforced only occasionally and then usually because of some local incident. Gypsies carried on more or less regardless, and were frequently joined by non-gypsy outlaws and undesirables seeking comfort and friendship in a society of equals.

It was a risky business, though. As late as 1725 in Holland, some gypsies were tortured and had their heads cut off and put up on spikes to warn others away.

And so on. Things really didn't improve until the abolition of slavery became a general thing throughout Europe. Many gypsies had been made serfs and even the ones who kept travelling and plying their trades were usually regarded, wherever they stopped, as the property of the local lord to do with as he pleased. In some countries, Russia and Spain for instance, gypsies did well and were tolerated and even appreciated. In others, like Germany and Romania, they were fiercely persecuted.

By 1850 or so, it was at least possible and permissible in almost all of Europe to be a free gypsy, and apart from occasional upsurges of anti gypsy feeling there was only one more viciously serious attack and that was by Adolf Hitler, who sent many thousands to their deaths.

In Britain there were many, many little local difficulties and almost universal prejudice and disdain, but the travelling way of life was feasible and it gradually acquired a kind of standard pattern and a romantic patina.

Gypsies could offer the rest of society certain useful and marketable products and services. These were:

Horses, and everything to do with horses: buying, selling, breaking, training, doctoring, shoeing, harness

mending and making, carts likewise, riding lessons, grooming and stable work. Gypsies and horses go together like cigareets and whisky and wild wild women. In a world driven by horses the gypsy was a much needed person, if not always properly valued and respected. Of course, as ever, there has to be a down side, and gypsy skills at faking and disguising horses for sale were as highly developed and as famous as their abilities to make a bad tempered horse good and a lazy horse lively.

Metal working and smithing: although some European gypsies became metal artists, highly skilled in gold and silver smithing, British gypsies did not. They were known for tinkering with pots and pans, a trade which seemed to lead naturally into scrap metal collecting as the tinker became redundant.

Farm work: haymaking, harvesting, potato, pea, fruit

and hop picking, and other seasonal labouring jobs the whole family could do. Farmers also valued the gypsy's eye for stock and his doctoring skills with the old remedies.

General odd jobbery: things could be mended, painted, sharpened, cleared away, replaced. If the gypsies were in the village, anything broken could be fixed by the men — the vicar's umbrella or the widow's picture of her late husband — and the women could sell their families' output of clothes pegs and lucky charms.

Entertainment: in other European countries this was perhaps more important than in Britain. Over there they had dancing bears, jugglers, acrobats, and they still have gypsy violins (even whole orchestras in Hungary) and beautiful dark-eyed girls swooping around the place with swirling skirts, castanets and flashes of bare brown limb. While their legacy is

Django Reinhardt, Manitas da Plata and flamenco, we in Britain seemed to have ended up with the gypsy showmen and their fairground rides.

Magic: fortune telling came with the very first gypsies from India, and it was logical enough to diversify into spells, curses and potions with attendant talismans, and to bring in whatever sales aids might improve the act, like crystal balls, tarot cards, palmistry, bump-feeling and so on. It should be noted that no gypsy ever tells the fortune of another gypsy, from the lines on the palm or anywhere else.

All of these skills, crafts and ways of making cash have two things in common. They are transferable, that is to say you can do them anywhere. And they require the amount and kind of tools which can be carried about in a caravan.

Also, they are the sorts of services which are useful

everywhere, but in small communities only for part of the time. Few villages could sustain a permanent practitioner.

The gypsies turn up, they mend the village pans, knock up a few stools and chairs, train the two horses and the dog that need it, sell someone a cart, buy whatever rags and scrap metal there might be, pick whatever fruit or vegetable might be in season, and then move on. Next year, they turn up again at about the same time.

British gypsies, in the life they developed in kinder times, let's say very roughly 1800 to 1950, had their routines. Families and groups did not wander everywhere, but usually followed a circuit in a locality which they knew well and said they lived in. Gypsies thought of themselves as from the New Forest, or north Yorkshire, or wherever. They might dive off for the Derby and

Appleby New Fair, but otherwise they kept to the route that the family or small tribe had established as theirs. The villagers expected them to arrive, and when they did, business was done.

Now there is no need of such crafts and services. We don't mend pans any more, and we don't want a penny for a rag bag, and our potatoes are picked by machine.

The horse job is dead, apart from horse riding for fun, and even the most conservative farmer will usually have more faith in the vet's antibiotics than the gypsy's herbs.

There are still a few productive occupations which suit the traditional marketing approach; hit and move on. On Fair Hill, look among the trucks and vans and you can see which they are. Lee Brothers, Roofing Contractors. R Boswell & Son, Asphalting. Pinfold & Shaw, Painters and Decorators. Loft and Cavity Wall Insulation, Landscape Gardening, these are the modern professions of the wanderer who has more or less settled down.

Instead of shoeing your horse, mending your jam pan, selling you a few clothes pegs and liberating one of your chickens to line the iron pot, the new generation will asphalt your drive (and your neighbour's) then go down to the Moti Mohal for Chicken Tikka Masala in an aluminium tray.

Those gypsies still travelling tend to be in scrap metal, or maybe knocking for bric a brac, garden furniture, bits and pieces. Times are hard in that game. Mugs who know not the value of their old possessions are getting fewer.

Often the traditional gypsy expertise in horse-dealing and skills in metal-working have been combined to create a new career avenue in the fascinating and foggy world of second-hand motor vehicles.

So, what remains of the people who left India a thousand years ago? There are handsome, dark haired women still who like to wear bright colours with black, and who state their place in society with the amount and splendour of their gold jewellery. There are living-wagons done up to the maximum level of luxury, with more ornaments than a Victorian front parlour and more chrome than a dozen old Cadillacs.

There are men with hats and waistcoats who are never without the wherewithal to deal, whether that's a thick wad in the pocket or a solid gold ring weighing several ounces on the finger. They are also never without a nutmeg and a bootlace; a horse loves the smell of nutmeg, and will follow you anywhere with a bootlace tied around its tongue.

The old values are still there: display your wealth, improve your possessions to the utmost, know a few things the others don't. But are there any proper gypsies, and is there a proper way of life any more?

There are some with more gypsy blood than others, and the ones with more will say they are better than the ones with less. The ones with less will say it's more a matter of attitude than blood. So long as you're a Romani rai, a true didikai, you're a gypsy because you believe you are the lord (rai) of all you survey, and you're the sort who, without polish or great literacy, can always manage something (didikai, rough and ready type).

You might even find that some of the gadje are kushti, and the occasional gadjo might think you're not a bad old mush yourself. But if you're a traveller, and live as a traveller, you automatically maintain the difference and with it the prejudice and the reputation.

There are gypsies all over the world, in America, Australia and still in India where they started out. Funnily enough, there are very few in Ireland. The Irish tinkers, not from the same origins as gypsies but with a very similar philosophy, have rather more invaded the UK than British gypsies have gone over there.

Certainly in this country, whether you are proper gypsy, Irish tinker, New Age dole collector, conscientious refugee from the system or Fellow of the Worshipful Company of Didikais and Two Fingered Gesturers, it is no longer possible to turn up anywhere and any time you like and camp for a week or two.

Permanent gypsy sites have been tried, and somewhere succeeded and somewhere failed. You can be quite sure that if such sites were in any way desirable to the gadje, they would soon be taken away, and so that in the long term doesn't look hopeful.

No single strand of change in society can be identified as the one that caught the gypsies. We can blame the increase in regulation to the point where rules of themselves beget so many more rules that there is always a bucket full to throw at the gypsies. Big Acts, like the Town and Country Planning Acts of 1947 and 62, and the Highways Act 59, have little Acts upon their backs to bite 'em, such as the Caravan Sites Act 1960 and the Scrap Metal Dealers Act 1964. And little Acts have lesser Acts, and so do local authorities, most of whom are delighted to enforce every No Camping regulation but can't quite see their way to providing the camping sites they are obliged to.

We can blame the huge increase in living standards and in standardisation of life among the ordinary static population. As a person's wealth increases, so does his intolerance of those unlike himself in values and ambitions.

We can also blame the high-earning townspeople who have moved into rural Britain in pursuit of their urban dreams, and the country people who have increasingly left rural pursuits for salaried employment in the towns.

Whatever the causes, the habitats for most of the wildlife of this country have shrunk, and the gypsies are no exception. And it's not just the physical habitat. It has become more and more difficult to sustain even the idea of a freeborn people, outside the system, getting a living by their wits and by turning a hand to whatever, moving around the country as they see fit.

The rural Britain portrayed by the old black

and white films, in which Alistair Sim as the vicar perpetually clips his hedge while Margaret Rutherford freewheels down the village street on her bicycle with a basket on the front . . . this was the sort of Britain which could include and cope with gypsies.

It could tolerate them.

Country people were never great enthusiasts for gypsies, but they did put up with them. Gypsies had their uses, live and let live, everybody deserves some respect and room to manoeuvre.

After all, there wasn't a lot of difference between ordinary, working village folk who drew water from a

pump and gypsy folk who cooked over an open fire. In the early 1950s, when this writer lived as a small boy in Sheriff Hutton, near York, we went to the pump in the street for water, and we went up the back yard to the outside midden for other necessary purposes.

Mother cooked on a coal

fired range. Although we had electric light our standard of living was basically long stretches of monotonous just enough, occasionally interrupted by sudden surges of plenty when a flick of bacon arrived in exchange for a favour, or father came back with a sack of pigeons.

Such a life was nothing to crow about. Nobody who lived like us could look very far down on the gypsies, and almost everyone in villages did live like us.

Of course, they don't now. A lot of them now in the villages are the sort who complain to the police about cows mooing. If they are townie-crass enough to do that, they would most certainly make a terrible fuss about gypsy washing being hung on a hedge, horses being tethered in the lane and people doing in a field what we used to do on a wooden seat above a midden.

As the system has grown and absorbed the majority of the great British public and wired them up into its information highways, so to be a member of an unchanging, non-conforming minority has become gradually impossible.

While the gypsy minority has had to retreat, viewing its fate with horror, it has cried out and bitten back. As the suburbs covered the country and every open space in every village was filled by a new bungalow, the gypsies once again were back in the 17th century. They could find nowhere to be gypsies and they didn't like it.

Even so, compared to the fuss made by offcomer Aga-louts when their country bliss is interrupted by the sound of a tractor starting up on a dark winter's morning, the fuss made by gypsies who didn't want their entire life to disappear seems minimal.

If there are no village pumps in the village, where does the nomad get water? From somebody's house. But if the high-nosed office worker washes the car on Sunday morning in the driveway while he refuses to give the nasty dirty gyppo some water, what does he expect the gyppo to do? Tug his flipping forelock?

If the travelling scrap dealer cannot stay in the lane for a few days until his flat cart is full, then he must stay on a designated site with many other scrap collectors for months and months. Is there any wonder that the site becomes a scrap heap? And the scrap heap, of course, cannot be tolerated.

Gypsies of the 1950s and 60s who changed from horse to lorry, from *vardo* to trailer caravan, and from free firewood to expensive bottled gas, did so mostly in the belief that they were only changing the means. What they were really doing was signalling the end.

THE APPLEBY RAI

My grandfather was a travelling man who married a woman with a farm. Quite how my grandmother got that farm, seeing as she was the youngest of 21 children, I don't know, but anyway get it and him she did.

He was an old man by the time I knew him, and a very old fashioned one. He was mainly responsible for bringing me up, which probably explains quite a lot. The war and various things meant that I didn't see quite so much of my father, and the man that I saw in his place was born around 1870 and represented an age that was going fast and nearly gone.

I say I saw him. I saw him when he was at home. He might have married into a house and land, but he was still a traveller. Travelling was in his blood, so he was always off somewhere.

Sometimes he took me. I have this particular clear memory of us on the cart, grandfather driving and turning into a terrace street in a big town.

Doubtless we would be collecting scrap or any old bits and pieces.

There was washing hanging across the street, like there always was in those days, and my grandfather was using his whip to lift it up as we went underneath it.

This wouldn't do at all for one woman who came out and started shouting at us, calling us gyppo and diddicoy and questioning our right to exist, much less our right to lift up her washing.

I tried to encourage us to keep moving but grandfather, who was getting deaf by this time of his life, wouldn't budge until he knew what she was on about.

"What's she say?" he shouted at me.

"It doesn't matter" I shouted back. "Keep going. It's nothing."

"WHAT'S SHE SAY??!!!" he shouted, this time in a tone not to be denied.

So I gave him a brief summary of her remarks, and he gave me the reins and got down off the cart and walked around the back of it. He went right up

to this woman who, to give her credit, stood her ground.

"I'll tell you what it is, missus" he said, evenly but loudly enough for the street to hear. "I am very sorry if I have damaged such as shirts, or sheets, in any way by my careless progress through them. But I'll just give you some advice if I may, which I learned from watching my own dear wife. And it's this. Do as she does. When she wants to hang anything out, be it on a line or over a hedge, she always washes it first."

My pictures of grandfather are all to do with horses and carts and traps, and deals and talk, and being in the yard with other men who came to see him. I was just a little chavvy listening and watching, and these seemed great men and great times to me.

Of course at first you only pick up half the story, but this doesn't stop you thinking you know all of it. A little learning is dangerous, but when you're young you think it's enough. Invisible gaps in your knowledge can't stop you trying to put life's principles into practice, on the model of the great men of your acquaintance. Such men would never let the chance of a shilling pass them by, and that was the attitude I had, just like them.

There was this old dear who used to call me as I went past her house, and send me on messages for her. She would always give me a penny or two and I was always glad to go. One day she gave me the call as I was going past with a friend. "Here" she said. "Come here", and she produced a kitten in a basket. Next, she produced a ten shilling note, which was a large sum and more than sufficient to awaken every instinct, and told me to take this kitten, that is to say, this little boy cat as she called it, to the veterinary surgeon.

The vet's fee would be nine shillings and sixpence, she said, and me and my mate could have thruppence each for doing this errand.

We were to go to the surgery, deliver the kitten, wait while the veterinary administered the required treatment and then bring the patient home to mammy for, I would guess, a lengthy and luxurious convalescence.

She obviously didn't expect me to know what it was that the vet would be at with this young tom, this little boy cat, but I knew alright. Not only did I know, but I thought I could do the job myself, every bit as well as any vet.

Well, I'd watched grandfather with bull calves. I'd seen him do lambs and pigs with rubber bands. I'd seen him do horses with his penknife. They were all basically the same, as far as I could see. It was an easy job. He would never have dreamed of getting a vet in to do such work. He always reckoned he could do it with his teeth if he wanted.

Of course there was no time for the slower, rubber band method with this cat. We had to do it the most direct way. So, I just required a sharp knife, of which there was always one in my pocket, plus a steady hand and a bit of nerve and confidence, and that was it.

I said to my mate that I could see no necessity whatsoever for a veterinary surgeon, already as rich as Creosus, to be handed nine more shillings and a sixpence when he had more than enough and there were two definite cases of needy parties in the immediate area just at that time.

If my mate would kindly and firmly hold the little tiny kitten, I'd do the necessary, and the old girl would never know the difference.

Of course there was a difference which I hadn't bargained for, and that was the difference in size and relative co-operation between bull calves and cats. My mate was having a very hard time holding this little animal still enough for microsurgery, and then I remembered something else I'd heard in the farm yard and took off one of my wellington boots.

We stuffed the kitten in the boot head first, my mate pulled its back legs apart, I went in with the knife, and bingo! The cat shat.

It shat, not on the mat, but on my mate. The most amazing vertical fountain of liquid cat muck, with the power of a miniature fire extinguisher, zipped into the air and landed all over my young surgery colleague.

Well, that would be his job to explain to his mother how his jumper got covered in cat shit. Hell, he was complaining and mithering on. I put the kitten back in its basket and told him to something well shut his gob. At least he'd got five shillings in his pocket instead of thruppence. What was the matter with that?

Information is power, they say nowadays, and we'd had a bit of information and we'd used it. It might have been better if we'd had slightly more information, but there you are.

Information, knowing something other people don't know, is what it's all about. For example, my grandfather was asked by a wealthy man to get this horse ready for a show. It was a draught horse, a big one, but it was the slug of all time. No matter how fancy you plaited its mane and tied its ribbons and polished its harness, it still had no style, no flash. It was like it was stuffed.

No matter what we tried and however we fiddled about, it was nothing more than a statue of a horse. It wasn't a living, breathing creature with warm blood in its veins and a heart under its ribs. It was just a decorated dummy.

This was no good to us. The owner believed in the horse and, more important for the family income, he believed in my grandfather. We were expected to get the red rosette. Something had to be done.

"Nip into the house" my grandfather said to me, "and get me them snuff bellows. And see your grandmother and ask her for a small handful of ginger powder."

So grandmother wrapped me the ginger up in a twist of newspaper, and I got the snuff bellows. I don't exactly know what snuff bellows are for, but these were a small set of bellows, like a model of the full scale thing. I should think they were to do with snuffing things out rather than taking snuff, but what grandfather had in mind was more to do with snuff as in spicy tobacco than with snuff as in candlelight.

We got to the show and when it was approaching time to go in the ring, grandfather asked me for the bellows and the ginger. He opened the little instrument up wide, filling it with air, then poured the ginger powder down the spout. After a quick look round he went up to the horse's behind, shoved the bellows in its arsehole and with a flick of his wrists blew in the ginger.

Nothing happened for a few seconds, then the horse went rigid. It stood, all four legs stiff and splayed like something out of the cartoons. It never moved a muscle. Then, after a few minutes had passed, it began to step about a bit, and toss its head, and generally put a stir on.

It wasn't long before that horse was in one hell of a good mood. Talk about pacing! We were called to the ring and that great slug went in there like a top trotting horse, all spirit and flash, its forelegs going like the Tiller Girls. What a stylist! It showed those judges what a very fine animal it was, tossing its head at them and saying "Overlook me if you dare!" Of course it was dressed up to its best, and no horse could have had a finer rig, but it needed more than that. It needed mettle, and it was showing such mettle like you never saw in a showring before.

It won its class, and then it won the best in the show, and its owner's smile was a mile wide.

"You certainly know your horses" he said to my grandfather.

"I certainly do" the old man replied, with the merest touch of a wink to me. "I certainly do that."

Grandfather showed me that knowledge again with another slug of a horse. It must have been around about the same time because I was just a lad but old enough to be given a job. I was carting muck, piled sky high on the wagon, when this stupid animal we had at the time came to some soft ground and just stopped.

There was nothing I could do which would make that horse move. I called it every name I'd heard the men use, which was language most unfit for a young boy, and I cracked it with a stick, and I pleaded with it and I pulled it and cursed it. Nothing.

Grandfather, who had obviously been watching for some time, suddenly appeared beside me and told me to go back to the yard and bring out the old mare who was just finishing working doing something else. Now, she was a workhorse, was that mare. Feet like iron and a will to match. "And bring some chains" said grandfather.

We harnessed the old mare up to the chains and grandfather slung a noose of them round the slug's neck.

"You'll strangle him!" I said, but the old man just looked, as if to say, just you wait, my lad, and we'll see who gets strangled.

He unhitched the stubborn old bastard from the muck cart and shouted at the mare to get on. She pulled, and the other horse went down like dropping a stone. Bang it went, flat out on the ground. Grandfather shouted at the mare some more, and she pulled some more, and she dragged that other horse through the mud by its neck.

Only when grandfather was satisfied that the lesson had been learned did he let the mare stop and allow the horse to get up.

Meek as a lamb, it was led back to the muck cart, which was exactly in the same spot, and the horse was yoked up on the very same soft ground that it had stood so stubbornly on.

It looked apprehensive, you might say, wondering what was going to happen next. What happened was that grandfather stood behind and to the side of it and very gently, very softly, rattled a bit of chain.

That horse went off like the Flying Scotsman. It pulled that cart like it was a quarter full of feathers, not one and a quarter full with a towering load of wet muck, and ever afterwards all you had to do to get it to show its enormous capacity for work was to rattle a bit of chain, which was a useful feature when it came to be sold.

They'd never let you do such things to a horse now. Oh no, you'd have some idiot ringing up the RSPCA. But in those days you depended on horses. They worked for their living, and they had to work when you wanted them to. Different times, and all gone.

Just to show what age my grandfather came from, there was this Sunday night, years after these stories happened and not so very long before my grandmother died, and I was round at their house.

Grandmother was in her night clothes, sitting in an armchair by the fire, and we were watching Sunday Night at the London Palladium on a 12 inch black and white television that was in a cabinet. It stood on the floor. They called it a console model.

I was married by this time, and sure of myself, seen the Korean war and all that, and I had been into the kitchen to make grandmother a drink of tea.

I had to make it, because grandfather would not touch the electric kettle or anything electric. I voiced my opinion about this, how he would let her sit there for ever without a cup of tea just because he was afraid of a kettle.

Grandmother laid into me with her very best terms of abuse. Nothing wrong could be said about grandfather, and especially by a mere boy such as myself.

In the middle of this tongue lashing, the television camera switched from a picture of Beat the Clock to a shot of the audience laughing.

Grandfather leaped from his chair, banged the console doors shut, and shouted "You brazen mare! Sitting there in your nightdress and all those people seeing you!"

He never did come to terms with things that didn't have moving parts and you couldn't see how they worked. You could go further and say that in 1960 odd, when he was over 90, he saw the principles of life in exactly the same way as a travelling man of the last century.

If it was nothing to do with a horse or another animal, and if you couldn't buy it and sell it, it wasn't anything at all. There's nothing wrong with these values as such. It's just that they stayed as they were while the rest of the world went past and disappeared over the hilltop.

Such values, if you are to live by them, exclude a lot of things like pensionable employment, daily attendance at the same workplace, and time off according to a pre-ordained schedule. I mean, you might

want more time off, mightn't you? What if they got a rush job on and you couldn't get away for Appleby New Fair?

So, like my grandfather, I've never worked for anybody in my life. I mean, I've always done some work, but I've never been tied to an employer as a permanent thing. Never had a proper, long-term, full-time job, you might say.

Even in the Army I used to get away with it because I knew about horses and most of the men didn't, and there was always an officer who needed a horse training or treating, and this would be a greater need than the Army had for me as a sentry or a square basher.

Anyway, the nearest I ever came to work in the sense of full-time employ was in Wales. I'd been taken on by this certain member of society, a retired gentleman with more than one surname, to run his farm. Now, there was an agent there, contracted and salaried and with all the correct clothing, but he was as much use as a chocolate

fireguard and I found myself making all the decisions.

There was some good stock, a lot of good stock, all pure Welsh Black cattle and 500 sheep all Welsh breeds. And, there were some very good men working there. And they were good men. They would work.

I'd say one day, we'll get these sheep dipped starting at five tomorrow morning, and never mind any ministry man because he won't even have thought about getting out of his bed by the time we've finished.

And those Welsh boys would be on the spot, and they would work. So you see I was enjoying myself at this place. I could get things done my way, which is always something I like, and they would get done. No fiddle-faddle, no will she won't she and maybe tomorrow. Things got done and done properly.

The boss could see it, as well. He wanted me to come there as permanent. He offered me a good wage, and this great big house, far too big for us, and

kept wanting to know when my wife was coming down to join me, and I was very near answering all his questions.

Like I said, I was enjoying myself.

Then, one day, word came from the boss's wife that she wanted to see me. At the time we were having a complete check on the entire herd of cows, like an audit, all at the same time, something that had never been done there before.

There was a few with mastitis, a few broken bagged ones, and so on. I decided there and then to get a Limousin and a Charrolais, two bulls to put to the cows that weren't so good for pedigree breeding, so we'd get something out of them that we couldn't get with a Welsh Black. And there were more things wrong that we kept finding.

It had been badly let go, frankly, the cow business, and I felt I maybe should have done the job sooner, but you can't do everything. I had thought this agent was doing it and then I found out he wasn't.

This agent, with the tweeds and the latest in checked shirts and heather mixture ties, apparently believed that his official role was just to count the cows. If he got the same number two days running, well, that was proof of his abilities.

Anyway, we were in the middle of The Great Cow Audit and a lot of palaver when I got The Call. Her Ladyship would like to see me forthwith, or now. I sent word back I was too busy just at the minute but would gladly attend her at the earliest opportunity.

This message was not fully understood, it would seem, and another message came back. I had to go, instantly. There was no choice. She had spoken.

At that very moment, trying to keep my eye on the job and listen at the same time to this mush who was relaying unwelcome messages, I got pushed by a cow and fell on my arse in all the shit. Actually, it was worse than that. I was flat out, and there was more than just a wetting on that yard. It was deep. If I'd ever been able to swim I would have been doing the backstroke in it.

Looking on, my friends and colleagues, ever concerned for my welfare, gave me such sympathy and helpful advice as they thought necessary. I thanked them in the customary fashion, adding that if madame wanted to see me now, well, she could see me now. So off I went.

I have to tell you that the impression I'd had of this woman so far was not very good. She was arrogant, high and mighty, and a name dropper. She knew Sir Whatsit This and My Lord of That. In actual fact I knew quite a few of them as well, including an ex prime minister, several dukes and some of the richest men in the country, because I'd done work for them or deals with horses or sheepdogs or whatever. But that's by the way and I'd never have told her that.

However, this lady wanted me to be fully aware that she knew people of note and so I assumed that, as is usual in such a case, she was of no note on her own account.

The maid opened the door and in I went, smelling powerfully of cowshit. It was some house, was that. It wasn't a house, it was a mansion. It had suits of armour in the hall, parquet floors and portraits of the ancestors all the way up the stairs. It was that sort of a place.

I was shown into the library where Madame asked me about the smell I was emitting, and I told her that I'd been required to come at once, so I did, and here I was and could she kindly tell me what it was about because I needed to get back to work? Work, I told her, was what I was here for. I was not here for interviews in libraries.

What she said next nearly had me thrown on my back again. She told me that the Land Rover had been seen. Seen, I said? Yes, seen, she said. By all the village! And this matter had been reported to her. The Land Rover, in fact, had been more than seen. It had been observed. Observed, she told me, parked outside a public house!

Was it, I said? Well I never.

She said, it wouldn't do at all for Land Rovers belonging to her husband to be observed by the village, parked outside public houses. Such a thing was not to occur again.

I really wanted to tell her in very exact terms where she could put her Land Rover and her village, but I did have plenty of time for her old man and so I kept myself in check. I just said that I thought that everybody was entitled to a little life and liberty, and that what I did in my own few free hours was my affair.

Having the use of the Land Rover was part of my wages, from your husband, I said. Outside of working hours, which are long enough, and extra long enough, I am known occasionally to frequent the better class of licensed premises.

This, she should understand, would be for social intercourse and a modest quantity of mild ale, and sometimes also for business purposes. A lot of important matters are resolved in public houses, I told her. And if your ladyship doesn't like me

doing that, well, I'm afraid that is just too bad because I am not going to stop it.

Now, if she didn't object at all, I would be getting back to the cows.

As I left that room, in my mind I was off and away from that place. And that was the nearest I ever got to work.

What a contrast to some of the other women I've met while I've been earning an honest bob or two. For instance, there was the lady of the duck eggs . . .

I can say that although I've never been rich, I've never been hungry either. There's always been food, and it arrives this way and that. A brace of pheasants will turn up, or a rabbit, or a sack of potatoes, or whatever. Or, in this case, duck eggs, not being left on the doorstep but on the stove — but I'm getting ahead of myself.

I have always been very partial to a duck egg for my breakfast, and a woman I knew near home kept ducks and so I happened to be given six when I was due to travel up into the

Highlands of Scotland on a shepherding job. It would be new diggings to me so I didn't know what to expect in the way of scran, so I thought I might as well take my duck eggs with me. Then, if it turned out to be a clam-cat spot, I'd at least have my eggs to give me a good start off.

I needn't have bothered. The yard at this place was full of ducks, and geese and banties and every kind and any amount of poultry. I also soon found that the body who looked after the men's feeding was a really kind, nice sort of a woman except she did swear a lot.

When I landed she gave me tea, bread and butter, scones and cake, and told me that next day was an easy one for me. All I had to do was meet the boss, be shown round, and then I'd be ready to begin the job proper on the day following.

"So" she said, "there's no ***ing need for you to up so ***ing early in the morning, so you can bide your ***ing time with your ***ing breakfast."

All her conversation was like this, so I won't bother repeating it. You can just imagine the asterisks.

She asked me if I liked porridge, and I said I liked it very much. And did I like eggs? I did like eggs, and what kind of eggs did I like? Did I like duck eggs?

Next morning I came down and the kitchen was empty of folk. I'd done no work so I wasn't very hungry. A real breakfast comes at about nine or ten o'clock when you've been up and out and done a few hours, and you come back with an appetite, but if you're just getting out of bed at eight you don't want a great lot.

On the stove there was a vast pan of porridge bubbling away, and another pan steaming with six big duck eggs in it. The lads will be coming back soon, I thought. Should I wait? No, that porridge looked good. I'll just get mine and be done before they come.

So I got a bowl of porridge and took it to the table. Up there they don't eat porridge like we do, with milk and sugar on it. They put salt on it, and have another bowl besides with cream in, and they eat the two separately but together.

I like mine with the cream and sugar on, so I dolloped a few spoons of the thickest cream in Scotland and got stuck in. I was full, actually, when I'd had that, but as the cussing old bewer had made such a point about the eggs I thought I'd better have one, and it was very good with a slice of home-made bread and butter and plenty of pepper and salt.

I was just finishing my last cup of tea and sitting back thinking I wouldn't be moving just yet, when in came the old lass. She inspected the pans on the stove and said "Will you look here now! There's that ✳✳✳ing Englishman and he hasnae touched his ✳✳✳ing breakfast!"

Next time it happened that she did breakfast just for me again, it was porridge as before, just the same, a whole great panful to myself, but not duck eggs steaming beside it. No, this time she'd given me goose eggs, but in recognition of my feeble spirit and weakly sassenach nature she cut down on the numbers and only left me four.

I've been up to Scotland many times, and to Wales, shepherding mostly. I've lived in crofts for months on end, walking over thousands and thousands of acres and never seeing a soul, but that's not something I could do all the time, nor would I always want to be away somewhere so remote.

Of course if your knowledge and what you're good at is animals, then you have to be where there is countryside and space. They don't do a lot of lambing in Manchester, and I've never heard of the hounds meeting in the yard of the Piccadilly Hotel, so I'll stay away from cities no matter how much money there might be to be made.

Just the right balance of open spaces and people seems to be in this little corner of England they call Cumbria now, although it's really Westmorland, Cumberland, little bits of Lancashire and even, God help us, bits of Yorkshire.

Years ago we would always go to the horse sales at Hawes, which is Yorkshire, so you see I'll go anywhere if there might be profit in it. Twice a year it would be, and on the way we used to stop at The Moorcock which is Garsdale way, not far out of Hawes. We got there about ten o'clock. There'd be flat carts and horses and all sorts around the pub, and we'd be inside having a feed of ham and eggs, and some of them would take a good whisky or two, and off we would go to the sales.

Hawes gets very busy, and after the sales we would rather go a few miles back to The Moorcock than stay in town. Generally we'd be there at about three, and that would be that for the day and most of the night.

One year we turned up and the old landlord had gone. This new gadgy served us alright in the morning and off we trotted to the sales as normal. You have to remember that this was in the days of restricted licensing hours. Officially the pubs shut at 2.30pm, but they'd never taken any notice of that at The Moorcock, nor at any other pub I frequented.

So, back we went, and this gadgy says no, he won't serve us at three o'clock. There was about 20 of us, all ready to spend quantities of money between then and midnight, and he says no. So somebody told him about several new uses for his pub and we went elsewhere.

Well, he didn't last long, that landlord, not with an attitude like that, and then the word went around that somebody new had taken it over, and so we called in on the way to Appleby New Fair. No problems at all. Just like the old days.

The conversation was of horses, and in particular of one coloured horse that was the new landlord's.

Everybody tried to talk it up to everybody else, for the landlord's sake, but nobody would buy it because it had no feet, I mean, it had very small and very poor feet.

You know, I saw some long and lanky kind of a fellow on the television, an officer in the Blues and Royals or one of those, saying the first thing you look at in a horse is its head. What a load of rubbish. You look at its feet first, and if it's not got good feet, forget it.

Anyway, I was saying, we were having a real good crack and it was a long time after official closing time when somebody came back from the toilets and said he'd seen a police car in the car park. A quick reconnoitre established that there was indeed such a thing, in among the horses and flat carts and living-wagons and clapped out motor vans, and the proud person responsible for the aforesaid constabulary vehicle was currently in the other bar, engaging the landlady in animated conversation.

In five seconds every glass in that room was empty, except for one or two belonging to such as myself who didn't see why we should rush our beer for the sake of the police.

There was also silence in the room. There was tenseness. And then the communicating door opened and in walked the landlady.

"What's up?" she said. "Somebody died?"

No, they said, it's that copper.

"Don't you worry about him. Now, who wants a drink?"

Everybody got another, and later I just happened to get a quiet moment with herself and asked her what had gone on with the policeman.

He'd come to ask about a load of mud on the road and who's field it was that it was trailing out of, and she'd told him. Then, that business done, she saw him cock a moralistical eye towards the other bar where we all were. She could see that he was mentally licking his pencil. His foot, he thought, hovered only half an inch from the next rung on the ladder of success. Never would he get another chance like this, to book so many people all at once

So she'd just said three words to him. "Fair Hill lot."

And he'd just said "Oh, right, well, I must be off to see

about this mud" and disappeared faster than a rat up a drainpipe.

I don't know if it was the same copper, in fact I'm sure it wasn't, but a couple of years later in the summer I was driving a cart back home from a long day away. It was a good little horse, a good worker, but no doubt at all that particular day it had done very near as much as could be expected of it.

There wasn't far to go and we were trotting gently downhill when we were overtaken by a police car. He stopped in front of me and put his flashing lights on and everything, expecting me to pull in behind him. I just thought what a first class prat and swung out past him and kept going.

Next thing, he passed me again, and stopped, and this time he got out of the car with his hand up. We were still going downhill, so I swerved around him and carried on.

He got back in the car, went past me like a shot, and pulled up at the bottom of the hill. I went past him a little way, until the ground started to rise again, and pulled up. The copper walked up alongside.

"Are you blind?" he said.

"No, boss," I said, "I don't think I am."

"Then can't you see that this horse is exhausted?"

"Is it, boss?" I said. "Do you know a lot about horses, then?"

"And what do you mean by not stopping when I tell you to stop?"

"I'd very much like to have done, boss, but the thing about it is, this particular type of horse-drawn vehicle which you see before you, is of a traditional design and class which is not fitted with brakes as standard. So to stop while going downhill with a tired horse is against my better judgement, especially when I can't see any reason for my having to stop in the first place."

"Listen" he said, and he used a few short words, basically meaning that he had a fairly low opinion of the gype in general and me specifically, and that his merest and most whimsical wish that I stop should be more than enough for any such toe-rag as I obviously was.

I might indeed have been nothing more than the dirty beetle he described, scurrying about looking for something washed up by the tide, but I was also younger then, and I had a lot more exubriance. I got down off the cart and went up to this copper and looked up into his eyes.

"Look, officer" I said, except I didn't say officer. "If you want to make something of it, then now's your chance. Because I'm nearly as tired as that horse and I haven't got the energy to listen to any more of your nonsense."

It couldn't have been the same copper as in The Moorcock, because this one walked back to his car, took his cap and jacket off, placed them, neatly on the bonnet, and came back at me hard.

We had a right ding dong. All I can say is that he could never have arrested me on his own, but there again, I couldn't have knocked him down and got away. So we just had to call it a draw.

We parted on relatively friendly terms. He called me a such-and-such dirty so-and-so gype, and I called him a so-and-so arrogant such-and-such self abuser, and that was that.

It was well after dark when I got home. Hell, she was mad, was my bewer. And not for the first time, but what worked in my favour was the bruises. They bring out the best in women, bruises.

This is the great charm of the freelance travelling life. You never know what is going to happen, who you are going to meet or what you are going to see, and if you're driving a horse rather than a motor vehicle you are going at the right pace to catch on.

For another example, I was a bit off my patch, to tell you the truth, in the valley of the South Tyne, but I'd heard that certain opportunities might present a fruitful conclusion at an auction in Haltwhistle, so I thought I might as well make a trip of it. This would be about 1970. I took a good horse and the small flat cart with a few saleable items thrown on, and a bit of tarpaulin to see off the rough weather, except there wasn't any, it was boiling hot the whole time.

In fact I managed a bit of trade on the way with a farmer near Alston, so when I turned up in this little place called Slaggyford I had a bit of brass spare and I was feeling in need of plentiful refreshment.

I raised my hat to an old spinster of this parish and asked if she knew of any places of resort in her spacious and civilised town, and she said there were none. I found this hard to believe and, thanking her, quietly concluded that she was exercising high-minded control over the passing of information, so as to protect the moral welfare of a travelling man.

So I went a bit further and asked again, and was told by this other, even older but less righteous lady that she thought there was a pub at the far end of the village, near the church, but it might be closed.

In the mood I was in I could have opened Aladdin's Cave with a blunt teaspoon, so I went off at a flash trot and found this place and got the horse some water from the churchyard (there's always a tap in churchyards) and put him by the roadside. I gazed up at my unpromising destination. A clam-cat spot if ever there was one, but it was not in want of a name.

'The Kirk Stile Inn and Sportsman's Rest' it proclaimed above the door, and so without further ado I stepped inside.

The entrance door was in the middle, open, and through Slaggyford's dirtiest windows I could roughly make out that there was a large room on either side. Standing in the passage I could see that the room on the left was entirely full of stored materials of two types only: newspapers, and milk bottles. Old newspapers were piled to the ceiling, and there must have been a thousand milk bottles, none of them clean. There was nothing else in the room.

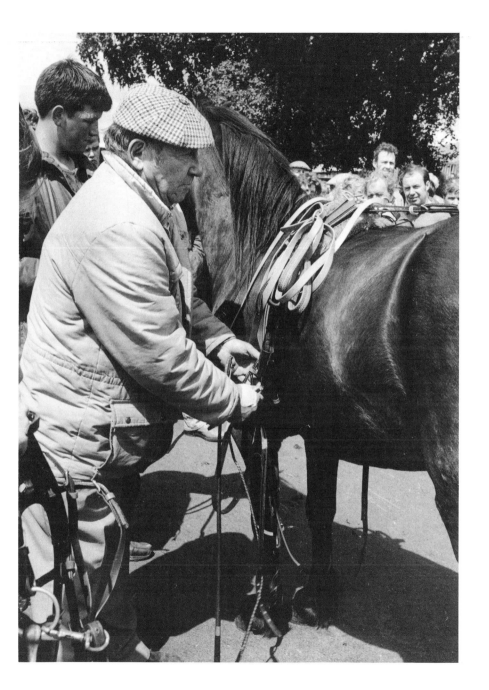

To the right was a room with a few tables and chairs but, as I saw when I entered, no bar. Then, this large, oldish man came shuffling in, dressed in a grey suit which you couldn't have sold to anybody. The trousers found the effort of covering his corporation beyond them, and so had protested in the only way they knew.

Through his gaping flies a shirt tail of uncertain colour could be discerned, and an odour of staleness and must seemed to accompany him.

He obviously expected me to say something, so I asked for a pint of bitter. There was none of this commodity available, it appeared, and so I modified my request to mild. This too was not listed in the stock inventory at present. Did he have any beer at all, I wanted to know? He had. He had Guinness.

So, I had a bottle of Guinness, on my own because he shuffled off. When I'd finished that I called hello and got another. And another. And later, another.

Four bottles of Guinness.
Not much drink for a drinking
man who's thirsty. So I asked
for another.

This could not be supplied.
Why not, I asked? Because the
Guinness at that pub was kept
for a man who generally called
in for a bottle on his bicycle at
about half past nine, and there
was now only one Guinness left.

This episode of The Kirk
Stile Inn and Sportsman's Rest,
Slaggyford, was a first for me
on several counts. It was the
first time I'd drunk a pub dry
on my own. Well, alright, it
wasn't dry in the strictest sense
with a bottle left, but I wanted
that bottle, and I'd asked for it,
and I would certainly have
drunk it, so it counts.

It was the first time I'd come
across a pub with just the one
regular customer. And, it was
the first time I'd ever been
forced to stop drinking when I
still wanted more, while the pub
was still open, and not really
minded about it.

Old boys like that hardly
exist any more, I mean, men
who simply do not care about all
the things modern people scream
and scratch for. Travelling or
stationary, such men are getting
as rare as fox eggs.

I was in this pub in Kendal
once, when there was a game of
dominoes going on. We were
watching and drinking and
having a crack, and I just
happened to notice that the old
boy who was winning wasn't
being very precise about which
domino he laid against what.

If it was fives and blanks to
go, and he had neither, he'd slip
a four on the five. Everybody
was talking and drinking too
much to see what he was doing,
I thought, but I saw, and I was
younger then, and when he got
up to go to the gents I had a
word with one of the players.

This was a new player, a
youngish man who I knew
slightly. He had just then
replaced one of the original
elderly four who had decided he
had better go home while he still
could.

The next domino game had a
slightly different atmosphere
about it, with my young
acquaintance watching like a
hawk, the central character not
noticing but the other two
obviously a bit curious about
something.

When the old man put a three
on a four he was pulled up for it.

"Nay" he said, sweeping
piles of pennies with one hand
into the other. He filled his
jacket pocket, tipped the board
and dominoes over onto the floor
with a tremendous crash, and
rose to his feet, puffing in a
dignified and measured way on
his pipe.

He looked with scorn at his
young fellow player and then
scanned the audience. His radar
picked me out and his lip curled
with a special reserve extra
contempt, as if he knew I had
grassed him. When he was
satisfied that he had everyone's
undivided attention, he spoke
again.

"Nay" he said. "If thoo's
gahn ti be til a spot or two, ah's
nut laikin."

("Nut" pronounced as in
butcher, not as in gnat.

Translation for those not fluent in Westmorlandian: "I am surprised at you, and it is beneath the dignity of a congenially liberal person such as myself to play further games with anyone so small minded.")

You're not likely to get such a thing happening now. Nobody would have the style to cheat so blatantly just for pennies.

Of course we're certainly not short of self righteous, interfering idiots, as I was at that time, when young and on this one and only occasion. The world is full of self-righteous interferers, telling us what to eat and what to drink and how to spend our time on this good earth.

I'll tell you what it is about time. Time was put here for me. I will decide what to do with my time and how best to fill it, and I don't need anybody, no matter how well educated nor how well paid out of the government purse, to advise me on this subject.

People are always saying they haven't got time. They can't do this or go there because they haven't got time. Well, it's a poor look out for them, because if they don't sit back and watch time and understand it and enjoy it, it'll all be gone before they know anything about it.

I'll tell you about someone who was a master of time. He was the landlord of the pub in a little village called Lothersdale, which is not very far from Skipton. Me and a fellow jack the lad turned up at this pub in an old van at about 6 o'clock, which was opening time, on a spring day. There had been a sharp shower which had passed, and now the sun was bright and as we drove up to the pub door there was this most beautiful rainbow. It was the fattest, brightest, best defined rainbow I ever saw, and the landlord was outside his door watching it.

We asked him if he was open, and he reluctantly came in to get us two pints. Reluctant landlords were not a new phenomenon to us and we thought nothing of it, although we should have because his reluctance was nothing to do with us being what we were.

We asked if he had any sandwiches, and he beckoned us behind the bar and showed us into a pantry. Flagstones on the floor, whitewash on the walls. On a three foot wide, two-inch thick pine shelf, what they would nowadays call a 'worksurface', whatever that's supposed to be because they don't do any work on it, they just open packets and stand the microwave on it, anyway, on this big shelf stood a massive white oval carving plate. Beside it was an old, bone handled gully, worn thin, and a matching steel to tickle it up in case being sharp as a razor wasn't sharp enough.

On the plate was the greater part of a whole boiled gammon, and this was a gammon from a big pig, a real proper pig, not one of these weasely things that looks like it was born and trained for doing the hundred yards. This gammon had pure white fat as thick as three

fingers and it looked absolutely great.

Further along the shelf there was a dish with mustard in, and a great lump of deep yellow farmhouse butter as big as a housebrick, and the butter was about the same colour as the mustard. There was also a crock full of new loaves of bread.

He pointed at all this, and at a jar of pickled onions, and at a tray of knives and forks.

He left us to it and we made the most magnificent sandwiches that ever were made, with thick shives of real ham with plenty of fat, butter spread a quarter inch thick on fresh white doorsteps, mustard, and pickled onions on the plate the size of golf balls.

Bearing our feast we returned to the bar. The landlord was absent. Oh well, we just got our pints and went and sat where we could look out, and there he was, sitting outside his door, in a chair, watching the rainbow.

I went back to that pub years later on a Sunday dinner time. You can guess what it was

like, car park full of sillinesses, pub full of snobby young men with too much money, all talking about the latest Soshidoshi 5.9XL and ignoring the lovely young women standing bored stiff beside them. They want to get their priorities right, these boys.

What do they want to go faster for? Which is more important, taking ten seconds off the drive from Skipton, or taking half an hour longer with a much cheaper, less dangerous and far more enjoyable form of sport?

It's like Appleby Fair nowadays. Most of what goes on has nothing to do with my grandfather's values. It's something else, I don't quite know what. There's a circle, getting smaller, of the ones who remember, and that is what matters to me, the annual reunion. Otherwise it's people who don't remember, don't care and don't want to know, and you wonder how long such an attitude can carry a great institution like the Fair. Not long, I'll bet.

CHARTERS

Whereas King Richard II on the 11th November in the sixth year of his reign in the year of our Lord one thousand three hundred and eighty two did grant unto the Lords of the Manor and to their heirs forever one fair yearly to be kept in the said Manor upon the fifteenth day of July being Saint Martin his day and so to continue for the space of seven days. By virtue of which grant and confirmation thereof from time to time we do openly proclaim, publish and declare that this fair beginning on the 15th day of July and so for seven days following except the Lord his day it shall and may be lawful for all and every person and persons resorting to this fair to buy sell and bargain or deal in any lawful goods wares merchandise horses geldings mares colts fillies beasts sheep or any other cattle whatsoever paying unto the Lords of the Manor by his officers appointed to receive the same pollage

package stallage standage and other duties belonging to him for the same.

And we do in the King his Majesty's name straitly charge and command all manner of persons whatsoever coming and resorting to this fair that they keep the peace during this fair and in the end so to depart. God save the King and the Lord of this Manor.

In the days before out of town shopping centres and hypermarkets, there used to be lots of small shops in the middle of all towns. These shops sold essential provisions, clothing and utensils rather than horse's head bottle openers, greetings cards and plaster of Paris shepherdesses.

Also, the older ones will remember, there used to be half day closing everywhere, and market day.

If you go back further than that, before shop-keeping became a trade of its own, shops were part of the craftsman's place of work.

The cobbler, the blacksmith, the glover, the hatter, they all had a lean-to or an extra room or space set aside where finished goods could be stored and inspected.

What we today might call 'the shopping' was done at the daily or weekly market and, once or twice a year, things you couldn't get at the market could be got at the fair.

Fairs were big business and as such were tightly controlled by the Tax Man, that is, the reigning monarch. Fairs were also highly attractive to everyone who thought there might be a quick shilling to be made by successful dealing, or by providing the ever gullible and sensation seeking public with a little excitement.

Fairs were therefore irresistible magnets for gypsies. Here fortunes could be told, side shows could be held, and horses, mares, geldings and any other cattle whatsoever could be bought and sold.

By the end of the 20th century most fairs have become nothing more than a collection of side shows. Travelling fun fairs are still largely owned and run by people with gypsy origins, members of the distinctive tribe of the showmen, but loud music, The Waltzer and goldfish in plastic bags, even if they are at famous events like the Nottingham Goose Fair, have absolutely nothing to do with fairs as seen by previous English kings looking to fund the public sector borrowing requirement.

Fairs have degenerated into this honky-tonk state more or less as the importance of the horse has declined, and the very few fairs that have kept something of their original purpose have done so only because the gypsies have kept coming.

The royal charter quoted above is not for Appleby Fair, but for the one held in Seamer, near Scarborough. For whatever reason, Seamer Fair is now just a small ceremony in the village street while Appleby continues in strength. Possibly Appleby was always bigger when the decline began and so outlasted its smaller fellows, but the disappearance of Seamer Fair demonstrates two truths about all such fairs.

First, as with Appleby, and despite all modern gypsy protestations, there is no mention of gypsies in the charter.

In fact, Seamer had two charters, one by Richard II (1382) and another later by James I (1609), and there is no talk of gypsies or their rights in either of them.

This is hardly surprising. Gypsies had not reached England by 1382, and by 1609 it was a capital offence to be one.

Simply to be a gypsy has been against the law in this country for 300 of the 500 years they have been here. Although the laws were

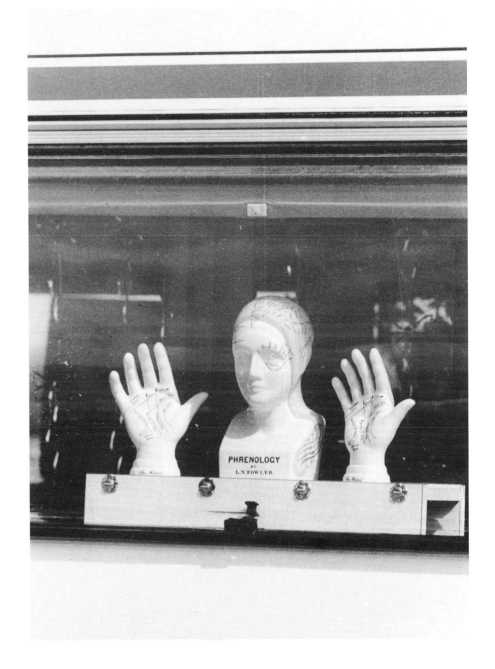

never consistently and rigorously enforced, they would be enough to give gypsies the status of non-citizen and therefore to ensure they were ignored in all official matters.

Whatever anybody says, gypsies were never given any special rights in any historic fair-granting charter in the United Kingdom, at Seamer, Appleby or elsewhere.

Rights or not, Seamer perfectly illustrates the second great truth about fairs, which is that they finally live or die by their gypsies. So, before we come on to the story of Britain's greatest living fair, let us look at the death of another, as told by the Scarborough Evening News.

17th July 1911
RIOTOUS SCENES AT SEAMER. VILLAGERS AND POTTERS DO BATTLE. Not for many years has Seamer Fair been marred by such scenes of rowdyism and misconduct as

characterised it on Saturday. There was an unparalleled outbreak at night, but also during the day as a whole there occurred serious injuries to several villagers.

The original cause appears to have been as follows. Two Seamer men entered the Londesborough Arms. Several potters or gypsies, visiting the fair, whose caravans were in a field at the village, were having a sing song. The two Seamer men were talking together and the potters called for order. The villagers did not comply and in the ensuing general scuffle the potters were ejected and allowed themselves to be conducted to their caravans.

Later, a body of 40 or 50 villagers proceeded towards the potters' camp at Manor Field. The potters hurled hot cinders and bricks, and 12 of their womenfolk, armed with iron bars, made an ugly rush at the villagers.

The villagers did not stand to meet the attack and the arrival of the police prevented more serious consequences.

(The following year, 1912, after the death of the 2nd

Earl of Londesborough, the Manor of Seamer was sold in 141 lots. The title of Lord of the Manor went with the ownership of a few small corners of land in the village)

15th July 1937

Since the reign of King Richard II Seamer has been the scene of an annual horse fair in July and today the fair, although smaller than the fairs of long ago, attracted a number of visitors and holiday makers to Seamer.

Mr T Harrison, to whose family the duty has fallen for centuries, read the proclamation. Seated on a white horse he was accompanied by Mr F Chambers, who has been Crier for 30 years. Mr L Rhodes, Lord of the Manor, threw coppers to the children after the proclamation was read four times. Prominent among the crowd were large numbers of gypsies.

15th July 1952

The horse fair proper has not been held for some years, but this evening horse racing will take place in a field near Seamer.

15th July 1954

Mrs Bamford, wife of the Lord of the Manor, said "It is the first time I have seen no gypsies in Long Lane on Seamer Fair Day."

15th July 1955

This afternoon a Baby Show will take place, followed by a Fancy Dress Parade, and village sports in the evening.

15th July 1959

Mr John Bamford, Lord of the Manor, said: "Once upon a time this fair was worth something. Cloth traders of the West Riding came to the village, and many other kinds of business were done, and the Lord of the Manor raked in a percentage."

15th July 1961

SEAMER REVIVES ANCIENT RIGHT OF TRADING AT FAIR.

There were signs of revival of the original purpose of Seamer Fair this year, when Seamer and Irton Women's Institute ran a produce and plant stall outside

the Memorial Hall, the original trading site. Mr John Bamford, Lord of the Manor, threw five pounds in copper and Mr Fred Harrison read the charter on a white horse.

15th July 1962

HORSE DEALER AT SEAMER FAIR

For the first time for many years a horse dealer attended Seamer Fair but he was disappointed for no horses were bought or sold, although the right to trade horses is mentioned in the Charter given by King Richard II.

Sitting on his gaily painted caravan, the dealer, Mr William Taylor of Preston, told the Evening News: "I heard about the fair and, as I travel about the country dealing in horses I thought it was worth a visit."

As the gypsies' interest in such fairs declined, so the fairs themselves declined. While arguments carry on for ever about rights and charters, it seems that the only true and important

issue about a fair is whether the gypsies support it or not.

It is perfectly certain that a large proportion of the population of Appleby would infinitely prefer a baby show and a WI stall, but for some reason thousands of gypsies will keep turning up every year, and thousands more gadje will keep on coming to goggle at the gypsies, and this despite a charter which is a mere 300 years old, unlike Seamer's which is 600, and despite a great deal of murk and mist surrounding said charter.

So, let's be clear about this. Charters establish markets and fairs but they don't keep them going. We can look at the origins of Appleby Fair, and very interesting it all is, but it doesn't explain why it is still here now.

Around the time that Richard II was granting his charter to the Lords of peaceful, Scot-free Seamer, the Earl of Murray and Lord Douglas were sacking Appleby and burning it to the ground. 150 years later, Leland wrote that *Appleby is the Shire town, but now it is but a poor village, having a ruinous castle wherein the prisoners be kept.*

Another 50 years, and Appleby is memorable *for the antiquity and situation only. It standeth in a pleasant site, encompassed for the most part by the River Eden, but so slenderly inhabited and the building so simple, that were it not by reason of the antiquity it had deserved to be counted the chief town of the shire . . . it would be little better than a village. For, all the beauty of it lieth in one broad street which from north to south riseth with an easy ascent of the hill: in the upper part whereof standeth the castle aloft . . . in the nether end of it is the church and thereby a school.* (The grammar school used to be in Low Wiend).

When this description was written, around 1610, there was peace at last with the Scots through the accession of James the First and Sixth. It was now worth people's while to build houses and barns and set about trying to make themselves as wealthy as they could, secure in the knowledge that it wasn't all going to be set afire by Border Reevers.

In the 1650s Lady Anne Clifford, Countess of Pembroke, built the almshouses and restored the castle and the two churches, St Lawrence's in Appleby, and St Michael's in the township of Bongate.

The Tuftons, Earls of Thanet, then came in to the castle and in the 1680s and 90s added extensions to it. About this time, 1685, King James II gave the businessmen of Appleby the chance to increase their turnover.

We will and by these present letters have given and granted to the Mayor, Aldermen and Capital Burgesses (of Appleby) and their successors a fair or market for the purchase and sale of all manner of goods, cattle, horses, mares and geldings . . . the said fair or market to begin in any year for all times at and on the second Tuesday in the month of April and to last, to be held and guarded for two days at any convenient place within the said town as shall seem fit to the Mayor, Aldermen and Capital Burgesses of the Common Council.

It is not clear what happened to translate the King's April fair into the June fair we know today. Research now being conducted into old Tufton estate records might provide the answer, but at the moment the fair change looks like a classy business move by the wise men of Appleby in the face of serious competition.

Whether it was because the Appleby fair was council run we do not know, but it seems that the rival fair at Brampton, origins obscure, overtook it in importance. In 1744, as part of the enclosure of common land, a certain part of Bongate Moor was privatised and it is possible that Gallow Hill, now known as Fair Hill, then became the site of Brampton Fair.

In 1750, under pressure and seeing a nice little earner, their April fair, withering and disappearing for ever, some kind of a deal was done and the capital burgesses of Appleby struck back. 26th October, 1750:

It is ordered by the consent of the Mayor, Aldermen, Common Council, Grand Jury and Commonality of the Borough that a Show of horses and sheep and also of black cattle . . . shall be from henceforth hereinafter duly opened and held in Battleborough on Gallow Hill and Brownbank within the said Borough on the first and second day of June, and also on the 29th and 30th days of September in each year except when these days shall happen a Sunday . . . and that the same shall be advertised in the papers accordingly to give proper and timely notice hereof and printed advertisements dispersed through the Kingdom at the expense of the Borough.

We find, 26 years later that the canny Common Council had no right to do this because, it turns out, it wasn't their hill! It was the Earl of Thanet's!

It is very hard to believe that the noble Tuftons took 26 years to realise that the biggest fair in the area was being held twice a year on their field without their permission. Of course the whole venture must have been agreed, and then something else must have happened to alarm Thomas Heelis, the Tuftons' agent and their man with his ear to the ground.

Whatever this was, it was enough to compel my Lord of Thanet to spend a few shillings on space in the Newcastle Chronicle of June 22nd 1776:

Whereas an advertisement hath lately been published . . . wherein a Parcel of Ground

within the Township (of Bondgate) and Manor (of Appleby) called Gallow Hill is said to be within the Borough and Corporation of Appleby . . . and that a Show of Cattle, Horses and Sheep would be annually held thereon; the words (within the Borough and Corporation of Appleby) have been falsely inserted, with an artful design that the same may be produced at some future time as Evidence of Right which never existed, to the prejudice of the owners thereof.

Artful? False? Strong words, and ones which would surely be vigorously denied by any local council of today. In those days, however, councils had to be put in their place by the aristocracy and no messing.

Notice is hereby given that the aforesaid parcel of land is a considerable distance from the said Borough and Corporation of Appleby and is not within it but lies in the Township of Bondgate in the Manor of Appleby and is the property of the Right Honourable Sackville Tufton, Earl of Thanet Island, Lord of the said Manor, and several other persons . . . who for the Convenience of the Public have permitted their shares to lie open, that the Show of Cattle, Horses and Sheep might be holden there.

It's not that His Lordship has anything against the fair. He just wants to make it clear who has the rights and, in view of its great success, the credit. A success it certainly was, for the very good reason that neither the hill's owner nor the upstart organisers from the council levied any tolls or taxes, so there was no pollage, standage, stallage, scutage, fruitage, newtage or what.

By 1821 the fair was being held on the second Wednesday in June, and by 1845 it was occupying three days.

Further expansion produced the current format of a week-long Fair, with its main business days the second Tuesday and Wednesday in June (except when June 1st is a Wednesday, in which case the second Wednesday is preceded by the first Tuesday. Got that? Who made up these rules anyway?)

Up to 1994, the Derby was always held on the first Wednesday in June, and horse drawn gypsies used to be able to get to the races and then to Appleby by travelling on the main roads. Motorised gypsies could do it more easily, and many did, but from 1995 the Derby is on a Saturday and so some choices will have to be made.

In any case the police seem to think that the trend is towards shorter stays by more people. More and more come to the fair but many of them don't stay the week, and there are arrivals and departures throughout.

Surely this can only compound the greater underlying development in the Fair. Its purpose for the travelling people was always

business, lengthily and subtly conducted, and meeting old friends to review the year, and making betrothals and other family arrangements for the future, and celebrating the fact of being a gypsy. Most of that is on the wane, and we are left with celebrating in a short, sharp bash.

There has been a grey band of change lasting about 60 years. At first the trend would have been difficult to spot, but gradually the horse became a form of amusement only, and the car, truck and tractor became the instruments of work.

Appleby New Fair followed the trend and changed with the horse.

There is very little real business done now. Few gypsies come to Appleby to make money. Appleby Fair is a form of amusement. The folk who make money, and who form the minority of the population of Appleby which is in favour of Gypsy Week, are the modern equivalents of James II's Capital Burgesses

— the shopkeepers, publicans, cafe proprietors and boarding house keepers of fair Appleby town.

But how can "The Happening", as the council calls it, continue to happen when there is no real amount of serious, money-making horse-dealing as the driving force?

The Fair is unique in the world. Some people in the town make a lot of cash out of it, and even if all the citizens together have to pay a price, the town's economy must be the better for the Fair.

If the Fair is to continue to produce the cash, then it must remain that attraction unique in the world. Therefore, serious horse business or no, the show must go on.

The fortune telling, the wagons on the hill, the horse washing, the picturesque characters, all of it must be there or people will stop coming. The gypsies know this. They know that their

annual week's holiday and chance to assert their gypsiness will fade away unless they keep their act together. So while the show used to be a side issue, now it has become the main thing and soon will be the only thing.

So, look closely at Appleby New Fair. The glory days are going. Of course the real glory days were long ago anyway, before the steering wheel replaced the reins, and anyone who wants to hear about them had better buy a few pints for a gypsy aged at least 60 and preferably more.

The glory is fading but our photographs, taken over three years up to 1994, were just in time to catch it.

Anyone setting out to do the same job in 2014 will have missed it. They will not be able to take such photographs.

Appleby New Fair by then will be for amusement only.